JAVA BASIC CONCEPT

CORE JAVA

VEERAMANI ARUMUGAM

Made with ♥ on the Notion Press Platform
www.notionpress.com

Java Class Notes

By Veeramani Arumugam

Index

Java Basic Concept:

Java is an object-oriented programming language that is widely used for building applications.

A **class** is a blueprint or template for creating objects in Java. It defines the data and behaviour of a type of object.

An **object** is an instance of a class. It represents a specific entity in the program and contains its own state and behaviour.

Java uses a **method** to perform an action or calculate a value. A method is a block of code that is executed when it is called.

Java has a set of primitive data types that represent single values, such as integers, floating-point numbers, and Boolean values. It also has reference data types, which are variables that reference objects in memory.

Java has a strict type system, which means that every variable and expression has a specific type that must be correct.

Java uses an **exception** handling mechanism to handle runtime errors and other exceptional events.

Java has a **garbage** collector that automatically frees up memory that is no longer being used by the program

Java has several control statements that allow you to control the flow of your program, including if statements, switch statements, and for loops.

Java has a powerful set of operators that allow you to perform operations on variables and expressions. These include arithmetic operators, assignment operators, and comparison operators.

Java has a number of built-in classes and interfaces that provide useful functionality, such as the String class for working with strings, the Scanner class for reading input from the user, and the List interface for working with lists.

Java has a rich set of APIs (Application Programming Interfaces) that provide access to a wide range of functionality, including networking, database access, and XML processing.

Object-oriented programming:

Object-oriented programming (OOP) is a programming paradigm that represents concepts as "objects" that have data fields (attributes that describe the object) and behaviours (methods that perform actions with or on the object). OOP allows you to create "classes" that define objects, as well as inheritance and polymorphism to help you reuse and modify code.

```
public class Dog {

// attributes (instance variables)

String breed;

int age;

String name;

// constructor

public Dog(String breed, int age, String name) {

this.breed = breed;

this.age = age;

this.name = name;

}

// method

public void bark() {

System.out.println("Woof!");

}

}
```


```
public class Dog {

// attributes (instance variables)

String breed;

int age;

String name;

// constructor

public Dog(String breed, int age, String name) {
```

this.breed = breed;

this.age = age;

this.name = name;

}

// method

public void bark() {

System.out.println("Woof!");

}

}

To use this class, you would create an instance of the Dog class like this:

Dog myDog = new Dog("Labrador", 5, "Buddy");

You can access the attributes of the myDog object using the dot notation, like this:

System.out.println(myDog.breed); // prints "Labrador"

System.out.println(myDog.age); // prints 5

System.out.println(myDog.name); // prints "Buddy"

You can also call the bark() method on the myDog object like this:

myDog.bark(); // prints "Woof!"

Class

In Java, a class is a template for creating objects. It defines

the data and behavior of a type of object.

You can think of a class as a blueprint for an object.

Here is a simple example of a class in Java:

public class Dog {

// attributes (instance variables)

String breed;

int age;

```
String name;

// constructor

public Dog(String breed, int age, String name) {

this.breed = breed;

this.age = age;

this.name = name;

}

// method

public void bark() {

System.out.println("Woof!");

}

}
```

To use this class, you would create an instance of the Dog class like this:

```
Dog myDog = new Dog("Labrador", 5, "Buddy");
```

You can access the attributes of the myDog object using the dot notation, like this:

```
System.out.println(myDog.breed); // prints "Labrador"

System.out.println(myDog.age); // prints 5

System.out.println(myDog.name); // prints "Buddy"
```

You can also call the bark() method on the myDog object like this:

```
myDog.bark(); // prints "Woof!"
```

In Java, an exception is an event that occurs during the execution of a program that disrupts the normal flow of instructions.

Encapsulation:

Encapsulation is a principle of object-oriented programming that refers to the bundling of data and methods that operate on that data within a single unit, or object. Encapsulation helps to reduce complexity and improve reusability by allowing developers to abstract away implementation details and only expose a necessary and simplified interface to the users of the object.

Here is an example of encapsulation in Java:

```
public class BankAccount {
private double balance;
public BankAccount(double balance) {
this.balance = balance;
}
public void deposit(double amount) {
balance += amount;
}
public void withdraw(double amount) {
balance -= amount;
}
public double getBalance() {
return balance;
}
}
```

In this example, the BankAccount class encapsulates the data (the balance field) and the methods (deposit(), withdraw(), and getBalance()) that operate on that data within a single unit. The balance field is marked as private, which means that it can only be accessed directly by other methods within the BankAccount class. This helps to protect the data from being manipulated in unintended ways.

The deposit() and withdraw() methods allow the user of the BankAccount object to modify the balance, but they do not allow the user to directly access or set the value of the balance field. The getBalance() method allows the user to retrieve the current balance of the account, but does not allow the user to modify the balance.

This encapsulation of data and methods within the BankAccount class provides a simple and secure interface for interacting with bank accounts, while abstracting away the implementation details of how the balance is tracked and modified.

Exceptions

Exceptions are often caused by errors, such as trying to access a file that doesn't exist or trying to divide a number by zero.

Exception handling is the process of responding to and handling exceptions that occur during the execution of a program.

In Java, you can use try-catch blocks to handle exceptions.

Here is an example of how to use a try-catch block in Java:

```
try {
// code that may throw an exception
int x = 5 / 0;
} catch (Exception e) {
// code to handle the exception
System.out.println("An exception occurred: " + e.getMessage());
}
```

In this example, the code in the try block attempts to divide 5 by 0, which will throw an exception.

The exception is caught by the catch block, which prints a message to the console.

You can also specify multiple catch blocks to handle different types of exceptions separately. For example:

```
try {
// code that may throw an exception
int x = 5 / 0;
} catch (ArithmeticException e) {
// code to handle arithmetic exceptions
System.out.println("An arithmetic exception occurred: " + e.getMessage());
} catch (Exception e) {
// code to handle other exceptions
System.out.println("An exception occurred: " + e.getMessage());
}
```

In this example, the catch block for ArithmeticException will handle exceptions of that type specifically,

while the catch block for Exception will handle any other types of exceptions that were not caught by the previous catch block.

Exception handling is a mechanism in Java to handle runtime errors.

It allows you to specify code to be executed when an exception occurs, rather than letting the program terminate abruptly.

Here is a simple example of exception handling in Java:

```
public class Main {
public static void main(String[] args) {
int[] numbers = {1, 2, 3, 4, 5};
try {
// this code may throw an ArrayIndexOutOfBoundsException
System.out.println(numbers[5]);
} catch (ArrayIndexOutOfBoundsException e) {
// this code will be executed if an ArrayIndexOutOfBoundsException is thrown
System.out.println("An error occurred: " + e);
} finally {
// this code will always be executed
System.out.println("The try-catch block is finished.");
}
}
}
```

In this example, the code in the try block may throw an ArrayIndexOutOfBoundsException, which is caught by the catch block.

The finally block is optional, but if it is present, it will always be executed whether an exception is thrown or not.

If you run this code, it will print the following output:

An error occurred: java.lang.ArrayIndexOutOfBoundsException: 5

The try-catch block is finished.

Exception handling is a mechanism in Java for handling errors that occur during the execution of a program.

It allows you to handle the error gracefully, rather than letting the program terminate abruptly.

To handle exceptions in Java, you can use a try-catch block. The try block encloses the code that might throw an exception,

and the catch block contains the code that handles the exception. Here is an example:

```
try {

int x = 10 / 0;

} catch (ArithmeticException e) {

System.out.println("Error: Cannot divide by zero");

}
```

In this example, the code in the try block attempts to divide 10 by 0, which will throw an ArithmeticException.

The catch block catches this exception and prints an error message.

You can also use a finally block to execute code regardless of whether an exception is thrown. The finally block is optional,

and is usually used to release resources that were used in the try block, such as closing file handles or database connections.

Here is an example of a try-catch-finally block:

```
try {

int x = 10 / 0;

} catch (ArithmeticException e) {

System.out.println("Error: Cannot divide by zero");

} finally {

System.out.println("This code will always execute");

}
```

In this example, the finally block will always execute after the try and catch blocks,

regardless of whether an exception is thrown.

Exception handling is a mechanism in Java that allows you to handle runtime errors (called exceptions) in your code.

It helps you to write code that is more resilient and easier to debug, by catching and handling exceptions that might occur at runtime.

Here is a simple example of exception handling in Java:

```
import java.io.File;

import java.io.FileNotFoundException;

import java.util.Scanner;

public class ExceptionExample {

public static void main(String[] args) {

try {

// this code might throw an exception

File file = new File("myfile.txt");

Scanner sc = new Scanner(file);

} catch (FileNotFoundException e) {

// this code is executed if an exception is thrown

System.out.println("File not found!");

}

}

}
```

In this example, the Scanner constructor might throw a FileNotFoundException if the file cannot be found. The try-catch

block catches this exception and prints an error message instead of crashing the program.

You can also handle multiple exceptions in the same try-catch block by separating them with a pipe (|) character, like this:

```
try {

// code that might throw an exception

} catch (ExceptionType1 | ExceptionType2 e) {
```

// code that is executed if an exception is thrown

}

You can also include a finally block after the catch block to specify code that should be executed whether or not an exception is thrown, like this:

```
try {

// code that might throw an exception

} catch (ExceptionType e) {

// code that is executed if an exception is thrown

} finally {

// code that is always executed

}
```

Exception handling is a mechanism in Java to handle runtime errors (also known as exceptions).

It allows you to write code to handle exceptions that may occur in your program, separate from the main flow of control.

Here is a simple example of exception handling in Java:

```
public void divide(int a, int b) {

try {

int c = a / b;

System.out.println(c);

} catch (ArithmeticException e) {

System.out.println("Cannot divide by zero!");

}

}
```

In this example, the divide() method tries to divide a by b. If an ArithmeticException is thrown (e.g. if b is zero),

it will be caught by the catch block, and the message "Cannot divide by zero!" will be printed.

You can also handle multiple exceptions in a single try-catch block like this:

```
try {
// code that may throw an exception
} catch (ExceptionType1 e) {
// code to handle ExceptionType1
} catch (ExceptionType2 e) {
// code to handle ExceptionType2
} catch (ExceptionType3 e) {
// code to handle ExceptionType3
}
```

You can also use the finally block to execute code regardless of whether an exception is thrown or caught:

```
try {
// code that may throw an exception
} catch (ExceptionType e) {
// code to handle ExceptionType
} finally {
// code that will always be executed
}
```

Garbage Collector:

The garbage collector is a mechanism in Java that automatically frees up memory that is no longer being used by the program. It does this by identifying objects that are no longer being referenced by the program and reclaiming the memory used by those objects.

You don't have to worry about explicitly calling the garbage collector in your code. It runs automatically in the background. However, you can call the System.gc() method to request that the garbage collector run, like this:

```
System.gc();
```

This is just a request, however, and there is no guarantee that the garbage collector will actually run.

Here is an example of how the garbage collector might work in a Java program:

```
public class Main {
```

```
public static void main(String[] args) {

Object obj1 = new Object(); // create a new object

obj1 = null; // remove the reference to the object

System.gc(); // request garbage collection

}

}
```

In this example, we create a new object and assign it to the variable obj1. Then we set obj1 to null, which removes the reference to the object. This means that the object is no longer being used by the program, and it is eligible to be collected by the garbage collector. When we call System.gc(), the garbage collector will run and free up the memory used by the object.

The garbage collector is a Java feature that automatically frees up memory that is no longer being used by the program. It does this by identifying objects that are no longer being referenced by the program and reclaiming the memory used by those objects.

Here is a simple example of how the garbage collector works in Java:

```
public class Test {

public static void main(String[] args) {

String s1 = new String("Hello");

String s2 = new String("World");

s1 = null; // s1 is no longer being used

s2 = null; // s2 is no longer being used

System.gc(); // request garbage collection

}

}
```

In this example, the String objects s1 and s2 are created and then set to null, indicating that they are no longer being used by the program. The System.gc() method is then called to request garbage collection. The garbage collector will then identify the objects referred to by s1 and s2 as candidates for garbage collection, and will reclaim the memory used by those objects.

Note that calling System.gc() is just a request, and the garbage collector may not run immediately. The actual behavior of the garbage collector is dependent on the Java Virtual Machine (JVM) and the underlying operating system.

The garbage collector in Java is a service that runs in the background and reclaims memory that is no longer being used by the program. It does this by identifying objects that are no longer reachable by the program and removing them from memory.

Here is a simple example of how the garbage collector works in Java:

```
public class Main {

public static void main(String[] args) {

String str = new String("Hello, world!"); // str is an object with a reference

str = null; // the reference is now null, the object is eligible for garbage collection

System.gc(); // request garbage collection

}

}
```

In this example, we create a new String object with the value "Hello, world!" and assign it to a reference called str. Then we set str to null, which means there are no references pointing to the object. This makes the object eligible for garbage collection.

We can request garbage collection by calling the gc() method of the System class. However, it is important to note that this is just a request, and the garbage collector may or may not run at this point. The exact behavior of the garbage collector depends on the implementation and can vary between JVM implementations.

It is generally not recommended to rely on the garbage collector to free up memory in your program. Instead, you should try to design your program in a way that minimizes the use of unnecessary objects and releases references to them as soon as they are no longer needed.

The garbage collector is a component of the Java runtime environment that performs garbage collection. Garbage collection is the process of freeing up memory that is no longer being used by the program.

The garbage collector runs in the background and automatically frees up memory by destroying objects that are no longer being used by the program. You don't have to worry about manually freeing up memory in Java – the garbage collector takes care of it for you.

Here is a simple example of how the garbage collector works in Java:

```
public class Main {

public static void main(String[] args) {

String str = new String("Hello");

str = null; // str is no longer being used

System.gc(); // request garbage collection
```

```
}
}
```

In this example, the str object is created and then set to null, which means it is no longer being used by the program. When you call the System.gc() method, you are requesting that the garbage collector perform garbage collection. The garbage collector will then free up the memory used by the str object.

Keep in mind that calling System.gc() is just a request – the garbage collector may or may not actually run when you request it. You should not rely on the garbage collector to free up memory at a specific time. Instead, you should design your program to minimize the amount of memory it uses.

The Java garbage collector is a process that automatically frees up memory that is no longer being used by a Java program. This helps to prevent memory leaks and ensures that the program has sufficient memory available for its needs.

You don't have to manually invoke the garbage collector in your code. It runs automatically in the background, based on the needs of the program. However, you can request that the garbage collector run by calling the System.gc() method.

Here is an example of how to request that the garbage collector run in Java:

```
public class Main {
public static void main(String[] args) {
// create a large object that will be eligible for garbage collection
StringBuilder sb = new StringBuilder();
for (int i = 0; i < 100000; i++) {
sb.append("x");
}
// set the object to null, indicating that it is no longer needed
sb = null;
// request that the garbage collector run
System.gc();
}
}
```

Keep in mind that calling System.gc() is just a request, and there is no guarantee that the garbage collector will run immediately. It is up to the Java Virtual Machine (JVM) to decide when to run the garbage collector based on its own internal algorithms and policies.

Polymorphism:

Polymorphism is a concept in object-oriented programming that refers to the ability of a variable, object, or function to take on multiple forms.

There are two main types of polymorphism in Java

Static polymorphism, also known as method overloading, occurs when a class has multiple methods with the same name but different parameters. The Java compiler determines which method to call at compile time, based on the number and type of the arguments.

Here is an example of method overloading in Java:

```
public class Calculator {

public int add(int a, int b) {

return a + b;

}

public int add(int a, int b, int c) {

return a + b + c;

}

}
```

Dynamic polymorphism, also known as method overriding, occurs when a subclass provides a specific implementation of a method that is inherited from a superclass. The Java runtime determines which method to call at runtime, based on the type of the object.

Here is an example of method overriding in Java:

```
public class Animal {

public void makeSound() {

System.out.println("Some generic animal sound")

}

}

public class Dog extends Animal {

@Override
```

```
public void makeSound() {

System.out.println("Woof!");

}

}
```

In this example, the makeSound() method is defined in the Animal class and overridden in the Dog class. When you call makeSound() on a Dog object, the version in the Dog class will be called, which prints "Woof!". If you call makeSound() on an Animal object, the version in the Animal class will be called, which prints "Some generic animal sound".

Polymorphism is the ability of an object to take on many forms. In Java, polymorphism is achieved through inheritance and method overriding.

Here is an example of polymorphism in Java:

```
public class Animal {

public void makeSound() {

System.out.println("Some generic animal sound");

}

}

public class Dog extends Animal {

@Override

public void makeSound() {

System.out.println("Woof!");

}

}

public class Cat extends Animal {

@Override

public void makeSound() {

System.out.println("Meow!");

}

}
```

In this example, the Animal class has a makeSound() method that is overridden in the Dog and Cat classes. This allows us to create instances of these classes and call the makeSound() method on them, and the correct sound will be printed based on the type of animal.

For example:

```
Animal dog = new Dog();

dog.makeSound(); // prints "Woof!"

Animal cat = new Cat();

cat.makeSound(); // prints "Meow!"
```

Polymorphism allows us to treat objects of different types in a similar way, because they all have the same interface (in this case, the makeSound() method). This can make our code more flexible and reusable.

Polymorphism is a concept in object-oriented programming that allows you to use a single interface to operate on objects of different types. In Java, polymorphism is achieved through inheritance and method overloading or method overriding.

Method overloading is when a class has multiple methods with the same name but different signatures (i.e. different number or types of arguments). Here is an example of method overloading in Java:

```
public class Calculator {

public int add(int a, int b) {

return a + b;

}

public int add(int a, int b, int c) {

return a + b + c;

}

public double add(double a, double b) {

return a + b;

}

}
```

In this example, the Calculator class has three add() methods that perform addition on different data types (two integers, three integers, and two doubles).

Method overriding is when a subclass overrides a method of the superclass. This allows the subclass to define its own behavior for the method. Here is an example of method overriding in Java:

```
public class Animal {

public void makeSound() {

System.out.println("Some generic animal sound");

}

}

public class Dog extends Animal {

@Override

public void makeSound() {

System.out.println("Woof!");

}

}
```

In this example, the Dog class overrides the makeSound() method of the Animal class and defines its own behavior for the method (printing "Woof!"). When you call the makeSound() method on a Dog object, it will execute the overridden version of the method.

```
Animal animal = new Animal();

animal.makeSound(); // prints "Some generic animal sound"

Animal dog = new Dog();

dog.makeSound(); // prints "Woof!"
```

Polymorphism is a programming concept that allows you to use a single interface to invoke methods that belong to different classes. This is achieved by creating a parent class with one or more methods, and then creating child classes that override those methods.

Here is a simple example of polymorphism in Java:

```
public class Animal {

public void makeSound() {

System.out.println("Some generic animal sound");

}
```

```
}

public class Dog extends Animal {

@Override

public void makeSound() {

System.out.println("Woof!");

}

}

public class Cat extends Animal {

@Override

public void makeSound() {

System.out.println("Meow!");

}

}

public class Main {

public static void main(String[] args) {

Animal dog = new Dog();

Animal cat = new Cat();

dog.makeSound(); // prints "Woof!"

cat.makeSound(); // prints "Meow!"

}

}
```

In this example, the Animal class has a makeSound() method that is overridden by the Dog and Cat classes. When you call the makeSound() method on an object of type Animal, the version of the method that is defined in the actual object's class is executed (e.g. the Dog class's version of makeSound() when the object is a Dog, etc.).

This allows you to create a list of Animal objects that can contain a mixture of different types of animals, and then call the makeSound() method on each object without having to know the specific type of each object. The correct version of the method will be called automatically, based on the object's type.

Polymorphism is a concept in object-oriented programming that allows a single interface to be used to refer to multiple types of objects. This can be achieved through inheritance, where a subclass can override methods of its superclass, and through the use of interfaces, where an object can implement multiple interfaces and be used as any of those types.

Here is an example of polymorphism through inheritance in Java:

```
public class Animal {

public void makeSound() {

System.out.println("Some generic animal sound");

}

}

public class Dog extends Animal {

@Override

public void makeSound() {

System.out.println("Woof!");

}

}

public class Cat extends Animal {

@Override

public void makeSound() {

System.out.println("Meow!");

}

}
```

In this example, the Animal class has a makeSound() method that prints a generic animal sound. The Dog and Cat classes both extend the Animal class and override the makeSound() method to make a specific sound for each type of animal.

You can use polymorphism to refer to an object of any of these classes using a reference variable of type Animal, like this:

```
Animal myAnimal = new Dog();

myAnimal.makeSound(); // prints "Woof!"
```

```
myAnimal = new Cat();

myAnimal.makeSound(); // prints "Meow!"
```

This is useful because it allows you to write code that can work with multiple types of objects in a uniform way, without having to know exactly what type of object you are working with.

Polymorphism is a programming concept that allows a single object to have multiple forms. In Java, polymorphism is achieved through inheritance, interface implementation, and method overloading and overriding.

Here is an example of polymorphism through inheritance in Java:

```
public class Animal {

public void makeSound() {

System.out.println("Some generic animal sound");

}

}

public class Dog extends Animal {

@Override

public void makeSound() {

System.out.println("Woof!");

}

}

public class Cat extends Animal {

@Override

public void makeSound() {

System.out.println("Meow!");

}

}
```

In this example, the Animal class has a makeSound() method that prints a generic animal sound. The Dog and Cat classes both inherit from the Animal class and override the makeSound() method to make specific sounds for each type of animal.

You can use polymorphism to create a list of Animal objects that can contain objects of any of the subclasses (e.g. Dog, Cat):

```
List<Animal> animals = new ArrayList<>();

animals.add(new Dog());

animals.add(new Cat());

animals.add(new Dog());

animals.add(new Cat());

for (Animal animal : animals) {

animal.makeSound();

}
```

This code will print the following output:

```
Woof!

Meow!

Woof!

Meow!
```

Polymorphism is a programming concept that allows you to use the same interface for different underlying forms. In Java, polymorphism is achieved through inheritance, interfaces, and method overriding.

Here is an example of polymorphism in Java using inheritance:

```
public class Animal {

public void makeSound() {

System.out.println("Some generic animal sound");

}

}

public class Dog extends Animal {

@Override

public void makeSound() {

System.out.println("Woof!");
```

```
}
}
public class Cat extends Animal {
@Override
public void makeSound() {
System.out.println("Meow!");
}
}
```

In this example, the Animal class has a makeSound() method that makes a generic animal sound. The Dog and Cat classes inherit from the Animal class and override the makeSound() method to make their own specific sounds.

You can use polymorphism to refer to objects of the Animal class using a reference variable of the Animal type, like this:

```
Animal myAnimal = new Dog();
myAnimal.makeSound(); // prints "Woof!"
myAnimal = new Cat();
myAnimal.makeSound(); // prints "Meow!"
```

Even though the myAnimal variable is of type Animal, it can refer to objects of the Dog and Cat classes, and the correct version of the makeSound() method will be called based on the type of object it refers to. This is called dynamic method dispatch, and it is an important aspect of polymorphism in Java.

Inheritance:

Inheritance is a programming concept that allows you to create a new class (called the subclass) that is based on an existing class (called the superclass). The subclass inherits the attributes and behaviors of the superclass, and can also have its own unique attributes and behaviors.

Here is an example of inheritance in Java:

```
public class Animal {
// attributes
String name;
int age;
```

```
// constructor
public Animal(String name, int age) {
this.name = name;
this.age = age;
}
// method
public void makeSound() {
System.out.println("Some generic animal sound");
}
}
public class Dog extends Animal {
// additional attribute
String breed;
// constructor
public Dog(String name, int age, String breed) {
super(name, age); // call the superclass constructor
this.breed = breed;
}
// overridden method
@Override
public void makeSound() {
System.out.println("Woof!");
}
}
```

In this example, the Dog class is a subclass of the Animal class. It inherits the name and age attributes and the makeSound() method from the Animal class, and it has its own unique breed attribute. The Dog class also overrides the makeSound() method to make a specific sound (a "woof").

You can create an instance of the Dog class like this:

```
Dog myDog = new Dog("Buddy", 5, "Labrador");
```

You can access the inherited attributes and behaviors of the Dog object using the dot notation, like this:

```
System.out.println(myDog.name); // prints "Buddy'

System.out.println(myDog.age); // prints 5

myDog.makeSound(); // prints "Woof!"
```

You can also access the unique attribute of the Dog object like this:

```
System.out.println(myDog.breed); // prints "Labrador"
```

Inheritance is a programming concept that allows a class to inherit properties and methods from a parent class. In Java, a class can inherit from another class using the extends keyword.

Here is an example of inheritance in Java:

```
public class Animal {

protected String name;

public Animal(String name) {

this.name = name;

}

public void eat() {

System.out.println(name + " is eating.");

}

public void sleep() {

System.out.println(name + " is sleeping.");

}

}

public class Cat extends Animal {

public Cat(String name) {

super(name);
```

```
}

public void meow() {

System.out.println(name + " is meowing.");

}

}
```

In this example, the Cat class inherits from the Animal class and has access to the name, eat(), and sleep() methods. The Cat class also has its own meow() method.

You can create an object of the Cat class like this:

```
Cat myCat = new Cat("Fluffy");
```

You can call the inherited methods on the myCat object like this:

```
myCat.eat(); // prints "Fluffy is eating."

myCat.sleep(); // prints "Fluffy is sleeping."
```

You can also call the meow() method, which is specific to the Cat class:

```
myCat.meow(); // prints "Fluffy is meowing."
```

By using inheritance, you can create a class that is a specialized version of a parent class, while still maintaining the ability to use the common methods and properties of the parent class.

Inheritance is a programming concept that allows a class to inherit properties and methods from a parent class. It is a way to create a new class that is a modified version of an existing class, without having to rewrite all the code in the new class.

Here is an example of inheritance in Java:

```
public class Animal {

// attributes and methods common to all animals

}

public class Dog extends Animal {

// attributes and methods specific to dogs

}

public class Cat extends Animal {

// attributes and methods specific to cats
```

}

In this example, the Animal class is the parent class, and the Dog and Cat classes are the child classes. The Dog and Cat classes inherit all the attributes and methods of the Animal class, and can also have their own specific attributes and methods.

You can use inheritance in Java by creating an object of a child class and referring to it using a reference variable of the parent class type, like this:

Animal myAnimal = new Dog();

This allows you to use methods defined in the parent class on the child object, as well as any methods specific to the child class.

You can also override methods inherited from the parent class by declaring a method in the child class with the same name and parameters as the parent method, and providing new implementation for it. This is called method overriding, and it is an important aspect of inheritance in Java.

Inheritance is a programming concept that allows a class to inherit the attributes and behaviors of another class. In Java, a class can inherit from another class using the extends keyword.

Here is an example of inheritance in Java:

```
public class Animal {

// attributes and behaviors of the Animal class

public void eat() {

System.out.println("Some generic animal eating behavior");

}

}

public class Dog extends Animal {

// additional attributes and behaviors of the Dog class

public void bark() {

System.out.println("Woof!");

}

}
```

In this example, the Dog class inherits from the Animal class. This means that the Dog class has all of the attributes and behaviors of the Animal class, as well as any additional attributes and behaviors defined in the Dog class.

You can create an instance of the Dog class like this:

Dog myDog = new Dog();

myDog.eat(); // prints "Some generic animal eating behavior"

myDog.bark(); // prints "Woof!"

Inheritance is useful because it allows you to create a class that is a more specialized version of another class. In this example, the Dog class is a specialized version of the Animal class, with additional attributes and behaviors that are specific to dogs.

Inheritance is a programming concept that allows a class to inherit properties and methods from a parent class. In Java, inheritance is achieved using the extends keyword.

Here is an example of inheritance in Java:

public class Animal {

// attributes and methods common to all animals go here

}

public class Dog extends Animal {

// attributes and methods specific to dogs go here

}

public class Cat extends Animal {

// attributes and methods specific to cats go here

}

In this example, the Animal class is the parent class, and the Dog and Cat classes are child classes that inherit from the Animal class. The child classes have access to all of the attributes and methods of the parent class, as well as any additional attributes and methods they define themselves.

You can use inheritance to create a relationship between classes, where child classes can reuse and extend the behavior of the parent class. For example, you could define the eat() method in the Animal class, and then have the Dog and Cat classes inherit this behavior without having to redefine it.

public class Animal {

public void eat() {

System.out.println("Some generic animal eating behavior");

}

```
}
public class Dog extends Animal {
// no need to define an eat() method here, because it is inherited from the Animal class
}
public class Cat extends Animal {
// no need to define an eat() method here, because it is inherited from the Animal class
}
```

Abstraction:

Abstraction is a programming concept that allows you to focus on the essential characteristics of an object and ignore the non-essential details. In Java, abstraction is achieved using abstract classes and interfaces.

Here is an example of an abstract class in Java:

```
public abstract class Animal {
// attributes and methods common to all animals go here
// can include both abstract and concrete methods
public abstract void makeSound();
}
public class Dog extends Animal {
@Override
public void makeSound() {
System.out.println("Woof!");
}
}
public class Cat extends Animal {
@Override
public void makeSound() {
System.out.println("Meow!");
```

```
}

}
```

In this example, the Animal class is an abstract class that defines a common interface for all animals, including an abstract makeSound() method. The Dog and Cat classes are concrete subclasses that must implement the makeSound() method.

You can use abstraction to define a common interface for a group of related objects, without specifying the implementation details. This allows you to write code that is more flexible and easier to modify, because you can create new types of objects that conform to the interface without changing existing code.

For example, you could use the Animal class as a base class for a program that simulates a virtual pet, and then create different types of animals (e.g. dogs, cats, birds, etc.) that all have their own specific behaviors, while still conforming to the common interface defined by the Animal class.

Abstraction is a programming concept that refers to the ability to focus on the essential characteristics of an object, while ignoring the non-essential details. In Java, abstraction is achieved using abstract classes and interfaces.

An abstract class is a class that contains one or more abstract methods. An abstract method is a method that is declared, but does not have an implementation. This means that any class that extends the abstract class must implement the abstract methods.

Here is an example of an abstract class in Java:

```
public abstract class Animal {

// attributes and concrete methods go here

// abstract method

public abstract void makeSound();

}

public class Dog extends Animal {

@Override

public void makeSound() {

System.out.println("Woof!");

}

}

public class Cat extends Animal {
```

```
@Override
public void makeSound() {
System.out.println("Meow!");
}
}
```

In this example, the Animal class is an abstract class that contains the abstract method makeSound(). The Dog and Cat classes extend the Animal class and provide concrete implementations of the makeSound() method.

An interface is a similar concept to an abstract class, but it can only contain abstract methods and constants (fields with the static and final modifiers). An interface can be implemented by a class using the implements keyword.

Here is an example of an interface in Java:

```
public interface Animal {
// constants and abstract methods go here
// abstract method
void makeSound();
}
public class Dog implements Animal {
@Override
public void makeSound() {
System.out.println("Woof!");
}
}
public class Cat implements Animal {
@Override
public void makeSound() {
System.out.println("Meow!");
}
```

}

In this example, the Animal interface contains the abstract method makeSound(), and the Dog and Cat classes implement the Animal interface and provide concrete implementations of the makeSound() method.

Abstraction allows you to define a common interface for different types of objects, without specifying how the objects should be implemented. This allows you to create flexible and modular code that can be easily extended and modified.

Abstraction is a programming concept that allows you to focus on the essential features of an object and ignore the non-essential details. In Java, abstraction is achieved using abstract classes and interfaces.

An abstract class is a class that cannot be instantiated and is meant to be a base class for one or more derived classes. An abstract class can have abstract methods (methods without a body) and concrete methods (methods with a body).

Here is an example of an abstract class in Java:

```
public abstract class Animal {

// concrete method

public void eat() {

System.out.println("Eating...");

}

// abstract method

public abstract void makeSound();

}

public class Dog extends Animal {

@Override

public void makeSound() {

System.out.println("Woof!");

}

}

public class Cat extends Animal {

@Override

public void makeSound() {
```

```
System.out.println("Meow!");

}

}
```

In this example, the Animal class is an abstract class that has a concrete eat() method and an abstract makeSound() method. The Dog and Cat classes are concrete classes that extend the Animal class and provide an implementation for the makeSound() method.

An interface is a Java construct that defines a set of abstract methods that a class must implement. An interface can also contain constants and default methods (methods with a default implementation).

Here is an example of an interface in Java:

```
public interface Animal {

// constant

int NUM_LEGS = 4;

// abstract method

void makeSound();

// default method

default void eat() {

System.out.println("Eating...");

}

}

public class Dog implements Animal {

@Override

public void makeSound() {

System.out.println("Woof!");

}

}

public class Cat implements Animal {

@Override
```

```
public void makeSound() {
System.out.println("Meow!");
}
}
```

In this example, the Animal interface defines an abstract makeSound() method and a default eat() method. The Dog and Cat classes are concrete classes that implement the Animal interface and provide an implementation for the makeSound() method.

Abstraction allows you to design your code in a way that focuses on what an object does rather than how it does it, which makes it easier to understand and maintain. It also allows you to change the implementation of an object without affecting the code that uses it.

Abstraction is a programming concept that allows you to focus on what an object does, rather than how it does it. In Java, abstraction is achieved using abstract classes and methods.

An abstract class is a class that cannot be instantiated, but can be inherited by other classes. An abstract class can contain both abstract methods (methods without a body) and concrete methods (methods with a body).

Here is an example of abstraction in Java using an abstract class:

```
public abstract class Animal {
// attributes go here
// abstract method
public abstract void makeSound();
// concrete method
public void eat() {
System.out.println("Some generic animal eating behavior");
}
}
public class Dog extends Animal {
@Override
public void makeSound() {
System.out.println("Woof!");
}
```

```
}
public class Cat extends Animal {
@Override
public void makeSound() {
System.out.println("Meow!");
}
}
```

In this example, the Animal class is an abstract class that contains an abstract method called makeSound() and a concrete method called eat(). The Dog and Cat classes are concrete classes that inherit from the Animal class and provide their own implementation of the makeSound() method.

You can use abstraction to define the behavior of a class without having to specify how that behavior is implemented. For example, you can use the makeSound() method to make a sound without having to specify exactly what sound is made. This allows you to create a high-level interface for interacting with objects of the Animal class, while leaving the details of the implementation to the child classes.

Abstraction is a programming concept that refers to the ability to focus on the essential features of an object, while ignoring the non-essential details. In Java, abstraction is achieved using abstract classes and interfaces.

An abstract class is a class that cannot be instantiated, but can be extended by other classes. An abstract class can contain both abstract methods (methods with no implementation) and concrete methods (methods with an implementation).

Here is an example of an abstract class in Java:

```
public abstract class Animal {
// attributes go here
// abstract method
public abstract void makeSound();
// concrete method
public void eat() {
System.out.println("Some generic animal eating behavior");
}
}
```

An interface is a collection of abstract methods that define a set of behaviors that a class can implement. An interface cannot contain concrete methods (methods with an implementation).

Here is an example of an interface in Java:

```
public interface Animal {

// abstract method

public void makeSound();

}
```

To use an abstract class or interface, you can create a concrete class that extends the abstract class or implements the interface.

```
public class Dog extends Animal {

@Override

public void makeSound() {

System.out.println("Woof!");

}

}

public class Cat implements Animal {

@Override

public void makeSound() {

System.out.println("Meow!");

}

}
```

Abstraction allows you to create a common interface for different types of objects, while hiding the implementation details. This can make your code more flexible and maintainable, because you can change the implementation without affecting the users of the abstract class or interface.

Abstraction is a programming concept that refers to the ability to focus on essential features of an object and ignore non-essential details. In Java, abstraction is achieved using abstract classes and interfaces.

Here is an example of an abstract class in Java:

```
public abstract class Animal {
```

```
// attributes and methods common to all animals go here
// abstract method
public abstract void makeSound();
}
public class Dog extends Animal {
// implementation of the makeSound() method
@Override
public void makeSound() {
System.out.println("Woof!");
}
}
public class Cat extends Animal {
// implementation of the makeSound() method
@Override
public void makeSound() {
System.out.println("Meow!");
}
}
```

In this example, the Animal class is an abstract class with an abstract method called makeSound(). This means that the Animal class cannot be instantiated, and any class that extends it must implement the makeSound() method. The Dog and Cat classes are concrete classes that extend the Animal class and provide their own implementation of the makeSound() method.

You can use abstraction to define a common interface for a group of related objects, while allowing each object to implement the details of that interface in its own way. For example, you could define an Animal interface with a move() method, and then have the Dog and Cat classes implement the move() method in their own way (e.g. a dog might move by running, while a cat might move by climbing).

```
public interface Animal {
void move();
}
```

```
public class Dog implements Animal {

@Override

public void move() {

System.out.println("The dog is running");

}

}

public class Cat implements Animal {

@Override

public void move() {

System.out.println("The cat is climbing");

}

}
```

Constructor:

In Java, a constructor is a special method that is called when an object is created. It is used to initialize the object's state.

Here is an example of a class with a constructor in Java:

```
public class Dog {

// attributes (instance variables)

String breed;

int age;

String name;

// constructor

public Dog(String breed, int age, String name) {

this.breed = breed;

this.age = age;

this.name = name;
```

```
}

// method

public void bark() {

System.out.println("Woof!");

}

}
```

In this example, the Dog class has a constructor with three parameters: breed, age, and name. When you create an instance of the Dog class, you can pass in values for these parameters like this:

```
Dog myDog = new Dog("Labrador", 5, "Buddy");
```

The constructor will use these values to initialize the breed, age, and name attributes of the myDog object.

If you don't provide a constructor for a class, Java will automatically create a default constructor for you. However, if you define a constructor for a class, the default constructor will no longer be available.

You can also define multiple constructors for a class by overloading the constructor method. For example:

```
public class Dog {

// attributes (instance variables)

String breed;

int age;

String name;

// constructor with three parameters

public Dog(String breed, int age, String name) {

this.breed = breed;

this.age = age;

this.name = name;

}

// constructor with two parameters

public Dog(String breed, int age) {

this.breed = breed;
```

```
this.age = age;
this.name = "Unknown";
}
// method
public void bark() {
System.out.println("Woof!");
}
}
```

Now you can create a Dog object using either of the following constructors:

```
Dog myDog = new Dog("Labrador", 5, "Buddy");
Dog myDog2 = new Dog("Poodle", 3);
```

In Java, a constructor is a special method that is called when an object is created. It is used to initialize the object and allocate memory for it.

Here is an example of a class with a constructor in Java:

```
public class Dog {
// attributes (instance variables)
String breed;
int age;
String name;
// constructor
public Dog(String breed, int age, String name) {
this.breed = breed;
this.age = age;
this.name = name;
}
}
```

To create an object of the Dog class, you would use the new operator and call the constructor like this:

```
Dog myDog = new Dog("Labrador", 5, "Buddy");
```

This creates a new Dog object with the specified breed, age, and name, and assigns it to the myDog variable.

You can also define multiple constructors for a class, each with a different signature (i.e. a different number or type of parameters). This is called constructor overloading. Here is an example:

```
public class Dog {
// attributes (instance variables)
String breed;
int age;
String name;
// constructors
public Dog(String breed, int age, String name) {
this.breed = breed;
this.age = age;
this.name = name;
}
public Dog(String breed, int age) {
this(breed, age, null);
}
public Dog(String breed) {
this(breed, 0, null);
}
}
```

In this example, the Dog class has three constructors: one that takes three parameters, one that takes two parameters, and one that takes one parameter. You can use any of these constructors to create a Dog object, depending on the information you have available.

A constructor is a special method in Java that is used to create and initialize an object. Every class has at least one constructor, and you can define additional constructors for a class if needed.

Here is an example of a class with a constructor in Java:

```
public class Dog {

// attributes (instance variables)

String breed;

int age;

String name;

// constructor

public Dog(String breed, int age, String name) {

this.breed = breed;

this.age = age;

this.name = name;

}

// method

public void bark() {

System.out.println("Woof!");

}

}
```

In this example, the Dog class has a constructor that takes three parameters: breed, age, and name. The constructor uses the this keyword to refer to the current object being created, and it assigns the values of the parameters to the instance variables of the object.

To use this constructor, you would create an instance of the Dog class like this:

```
Dog myDog = new Dog("Labrador", 5, "Buddy");
```

You can access the attributes of the myDog object using the dot notation, like this:

```
System.out.println(myDog.breed); // prints "Labrador"

System.out.println(myDog.age); // prints 5

System.out.println(myDog.name); // prints "Buddy"
```

You can also call the bark() method on the myDog object like this:

myDog.bark(); // prints "Woof!"

If a class does not have a constructor defined, Java will automatically create a default constructor that does not take any parameters. However, if you define at least one constructor for a class, you will have to define all of the constructors for the class yourself.

In Java, a constructor is a special method that is called when an object is created. Constructors are used to initialize the state of an object when it is created.

Here is an example of a class with a constructor in Java:

```
public class Dog {

String breed;

int age;

String name;

// constructor

public Dog(String breed, int age, String name) {

this.breed = breed;

this.age = age;

this.name = name;

}

}
```

In this example, the Dog class has a constructor that takes three arguments: breed, age, and name. The constructor initializes the instance variables of the Dog object with the values of the arguments.

You can use the constructor to create a new Dog object like this:

Dog myDog = new Dog("Labrador", 5, "Buddy");

The new keyword creates a new instance of the Dog class and calls the constructor to initialize it.

You can also define multiple constructors for a class by overloading the constructor. For example, you could define a default constructor that creates a Dog object with default values:

```
public class Dog {

String breed;

int age;
```

```
String name;

// default constructor

public Dog() {

this.breed = "Unknown";

this.age = 0;

this.name = "Unnamed";

}

// constructor with arguments

public Dog(String breed, int age, String name) {

this.breed = breed;

this.age = age;

this.name = name;

}

}
```

Now you can create a Dog object with default values like this:

```
Dog myDog = new Dog();
```

In Java, a constructor is a special method that is used to create and initialize an object. It has the same name as the class and is called when you create an instance of the class using the new operator.

Here is an example of a class with a constructor in Java:

```
public class Dog {

String breed;

int age;

String name;

// constructor

public Dog(String breed, int age, String name) {

this.breed = breed;
```

```
this.age = age;

this.name = name;

}

}
```

To create an instance of the Dog class, you would use the new operator and pass in the required arguments for the constructor:

```
Dog myDog = new Dog("Labrador", 5, "Buddy");
```

This will create a new Dog object and initialize its breed, age, and name attributes using the values passed to the constructor.

You can also define a class with multiple constructors, each with a different number or type of arguments. This is called constructor overloading. For example:

```
public class Dog {

String breed;

int age;

String name;

// constructor with three arguments

public Dog(String breed, int age, String name) {

this.breed = breed;

this.age = age;

this.name = name;

}

// constructor with two arguments

public Dog(String breed, int age) {

this.breed = breed;

this.age = age;

this.name = "Unknown";

}
```

```
// constructor with one argument
public Dog(String breed) {
this.breed = breed;
this.age = 0;
this.name = "Unknown";
}
}
```

You can then create a Dog object using any of the constructors, depending on the information you have available:

```
Dog myDog1 = new Dog("Labrador", 5, "Buddy");
Dog myDog2 = new Dog("Labrador", 5);
Dog myDog3 = new Dog("Labrador");
```

Instance, static and method variable:

In Java, instance variables are variables that are associated with an instance of a class. They are defined outside of any method and are not static.

Here is an example of an instance variable in Java:

```
public class Dog {
String breed; // instance variable
public Dog(String breed) {
this.breed = breed;
}
}
```

You can access the instance variable using the dot notation, like this:

```
Dog myDog = new Dog("Labrador");
System.out.println(myDog.breed); // prints "Labrador"
```

Static variables are variables that are associated with a class, rather than an instance of a class. They are defined using the static keyword and are shared among all instances of the class.

Here is an example of a static variable in Java:

```
public class Dog {

static int population; // static variable

public Dog() {

population++;

}

}
```

You can access the static variable using the class name and the dot notation, like this:

```
System.out.println(Dog.population); // prints 0

Dog dog1 = new Dog();

Dog dog2 = new Dog();

Dog dog3 = new Dog();

System.out.println(Dog.population); // prints 3
```

Method variables are variables that are defined inside a method and are only accessible within the method. They are not static and are not associated with an instance of a class.

Here is an example of a method variable in Java:

```
public class Dog {

int age; // instance variable

public void setAge(int age) {

this.age = age;

}

public void printAge() {

int years = 7; // method variable

int months = years * 12;

System.out.println(age + " years is equivalent to " + months + " months.");

}
```

}

In this example, the age variable is an instance variable, and the years variable is a method variable. The years variable is defined inside the printAge() method and is only accessible within the method.

In Java, instance variables are variables that are declared within a class, but outside of any method, constructor, or block. They are associated with an instance of the class, and each instance of the class has its own copy of the instance variables.

Here is an example of instance variables in Java:

```
public class Dog {

// instance variables

String breed;

int age;

String name;

// constructor

public Dog(String breed, int age, String name) {

this.breed = breed;

this.age = age;

this.name = name;

}

// method

public void bark() {

System.out.println("Woof!");

}

}
```

In this example, the breed, age, and name variables are instance variables. They are declared within the Dog class, but outside of any method, constructor, or block. They are associated with an instance of the Dog class, and each instance of the Dog class has its own copy of these variables.

You can access instance variables using the dot notation, like this:

```
Dog myDog = new Dog("Labrador", 5, "Buddy");
```

```
System.out.println(myDog.breed); // prints "Labrador"

System.out.println(myDog.age); // prints 5

System.out.println(myDog.name); // prints "Buddy"
```

Static variables, also known as class variables, are variables that are associated with a class, rather than with a specific instance of the class. They are declared using the static keyword, and there is only one copy of the variable shared by all instances of the class.

Thread:

A thread is a separate flow of execution in a Java program. You can create multiple threads to run concurrently and perform different tasks in parallel.

Here is an example of how to create a thread in Java using the Thread class:

```
public class MyThread extends Thread {

@Override

public void run() {

// code to be executed in the new thread goes here

}

}

public class Main {

public static void main(String[] args) {

// create a new thread

MyThread thread = new MyThread();

// start the thread

thread.start();

}

}
```

In this example, the MyThread class extends the Thread class and overrides the run() method. The run() method contains the code that will be executed in the new thread.

To create a new thread, you create an instance of the MyThread class using the new operator. To start the thread, you call the start() method on the thread object. This will cause the run() method to be executed in a separate thread.

You can also create a thread using the Runnable interface, like this:

```
public class MyRunnable implements Runnable {
@Override
public void run() {
// code to be executed in the new thread goes here
}
}
public class Main {
public static void main(String[] args) {
// create a new thread
Thread thread = new Thread(new MyRunnable());
// start the thread
thread.start();
}
}
```

Overloading vs overriding:

Method overloading and method overriding are two techniques in Java that allow a class to have multiple methods with the same name. However, they are used in different situations and have some important differences.

Method overloading occurs when a class has two or more methods with the same name, but different parameter lists. For example:

```
public class Calculator {
public int add(int x, int y) {
return x + y;
}
public double add(double x, double y) {
return x + y;
```

```
}
}
```

In this example, the Calculator class has two add() methods with the same name, but one takes two int parameters and the other takes two double parameters. This is an example of method overloading.

Method overriding occurs when a subclass has a method with the same name and parameter list as a method in the superclass. The subclass method is said to override the superclass method, and it is used to provide a different implementation of the method. For example:

```
public class Animal {
public void makeNoise() {
System.out.println("Some generic noise");
}
}
public class Dog extends Animal {
@Override
public void makeNoise() {
System.out.println("Woof!");
}
}
```

In this example, the Dog class overrides the makeNoise() method from the Animal class, providing a different implementation that prints "Woof!" instead of the generic noise.

It is important to note that method overloading is determined at compile time, while method overriding is determined at runtime. This means that the compiler will choose the correct overloaded method based on the parameter types at compile time, while the JVM will choose the correct overridden method based on the runtime type of the object at runtime.

The Java Collections Framework is a set of classes and interfaces that provide various types of collections (e.g., list, set, queue, etc.) and algorithms to work with these collections. It is part of the Java Standard Library and provides a standard way to handle collections of objects in Java.

Collections Framework:

The Collections Framework is built on top of the List, Set, and Map interfaces, which define the main types of collections in the framework.

The List interface represents an ordered collection of elements that allows duplicate values. It provides methods for inserting, accessing, and manipulating elements in the list. Some common implementations of the List interface include ArrayList and LinkedList.

The Set interface represents a collection of unique elements. It does not allow duplicate values and does not provide any guarantees about the order of the elements. Some common implementations of the Set interface include HashSet and TreeSet.

The Map interface represents a collection of key-value pairs, where each key is unique and is used to retrieve the corresponding value. Some common implementations of the Map interface include HashMap and TreeMap.

The Collections Framework also provides various utility classes for working with collections, such as:

The Collections class, which provides various utility methods for working with collections, such as sorting, searching, and shuffling.

The Iterator interface, which defines a standard way to iterate over the elements in a collection.

The Comparator interface, which defines a standard way to compare two objects for the purpose of sorting.

Overall, the Java Collections Framework is an essential part of the Java Standard Library and provides a convenient and efficient way to work with collections of objects in Java.

In Java, the java.util.Collections framework is a set of classes and interfaces that implement commonly-used collection data structures. These data structures provide efficient ways to store and manipulate groups of objects.

The Collections framework includes several interfaces that define various types of collections, such as:

List: An ordered collection (also known as a sequence). The user of a List interface can access elements by their integer index (position in the list), and search for elements in the list.

Set: A collection that cannot contain duplicate elements.

Map: An object that maps keys to values. A Map cannot contain duplicate keys; each key can map to at most one value.

The Collections framework also includes several classes that implement these interfaces, such as:

ArrayList: A resizable-array implementation of the List interface.

HashSet: A Set implementation that uses a hash table for storage.

HashMap: A Map implementation that uses a hash table for storage.

Here is an example of how to use a List in Java:

```
import java.util.List;
```

```
import java.util.ArrayList;
public class Example {
public static void main(String[] args) {
// Create a new ArrayList
List<String> names = new ArrayList<>();
// Add some elements to the list
names.add("Alice");
names.add("Bob");
names.add("Charlie");
// Print the list
System.out.println(names); // Outputs [Alice, Bob, Charlie]
// Access an element by its index
String firstName = names.get(0); // firstName is "Alice"
// Iterate over the list
for (String name : names) {
System.out.println(name); // Outputs each name on a separate line
}
}
}
```

The Collections framework also provides several utility methods for working with collections, such as sort(), reverse(), and shuffle().

Overall, the Collections framework is a powerful and convenient tool for working with groups of objects in Java, and is widely used in many Java applications.

ArrayList:

An ArrayList in Java is a resizable array implementation of the List interface. It allows you to store a collection of objects in an ordered sequence, and provides various methods for inserting, deleting, and accessing elements in the list.

Here is an example of how to use an ArrayList in Java:

```
import java.util.List;
import java.util.ArrayList;
public class Example {
public static void main(String[] args) {
// Create a new ArrayList
List<String> names = new ArrayList<>();
// Add some elements to the list
names.add("Alice");
names.add("Bob");
names.add("Charlie");
// Print the list
System.out.println(names); // Outputs [Alice, Bob, Charlie]
// Access an element by its index
String firstName = names.get(0); // firstName is "Alice"
// Remove an element by its index
names.remove(1); // names is now [Alice, Charlie]
// Iterate over the list
for (String name : names) {
System.out.println(name); // Outputs each name on a separate line
}
}
}
```

One advantage of using an ArrayList over a traditional array is that an ArrayList grows automatically as you add more elements to it, whereas an array has a fixed size once it is created.

Note that ArrayList is a generic class, which means that you can specify the type of elements that it stores. In the example above, we create an ArrayList of String objects, so we use the syntax List<String> names = new ArrayList<>();. This helps to ensure type safety and prevent runtime errors.

LinkedList:

A LinkedList in Java is an implementation of the List interface that is based on a doubly-linked list data structure. It allows you to store a collection of objects in an ordered sequence, and provides various methods for inserting, deleting, and accessing elements in the list.

Here is an example of how to use a LinkedList in Java:

```
import java.util.List;

import java.util.LinkedList;

public class Example {

public static void main(String[] args) {

// Create a new LinkedList

List<String> names = new LinkedList<>();

// Add some elements to the list

names.add("Alice");

names.add("Bob");

names.add("Charlie");

// Print the list

System.out.println(names); // Outputs [Alice, Bob, Charlie]

// Access an element by its index

String firstName = names.get(0); // firstName is "Alice"

// Remove an element by its index

names.remove(1); // names is now [Alice, Charlie

// Iterate over the list

for (String name : names) {

System.out.println(name); // Outputs each name on a separate line

}

}

}
```

One advantage of using a LinkedList over an ArrayList is that you can insert and delete elements from the list more efficiently, since you do not need to shift the elements around in memory. However, LinkedList elements are accessed by iterating through the list from the beginning or the end, so it may not be as efficient for accessing elements by their index as an ArrayList.

Like ArrayList, LinkedList is a generic class, which means that you can specify the type of elements that it stores. In the example above, we create a LinkedList of String objects, so we use the syntax List<String> names = new LinkedList<>();. This helps to ensure type safety and prevent runtime errors.

Vector:

A Vector in Java is a legacy class that provides an implementation of a growable array of objects. It is similar to an ArrayList, but it is synchronized and has some additional methods for legacy support.

Here is an example of how to use a Vector in Java:

```
import java.util.Vector;

public class Example {

public static void main(String[] args) {

// Create a new Vector

Vector<String> names = new Vector<>();

// Add some elements to the vector

names.add("Alice");

names.add("Bob");

names.add("Charlie");

// Print the vector

System.out.println(names); // Outputs [Alice, Bob, Charlie]

// Access an element by its index

String firstName = names.get(0); // firstName is "Alice"

// Remove an element by its index

names.remove(1); // names is now [Alice, Charlie]

// Iterate over the vector

for (String name : names) {

System.out.println(name); // Outputs each name on a separate line
```

```
}
}
}
```

One advantage of using a Vector over an ArrayList is that it is synchronized, which means that it is thread-safe and can be used in multithreaded environments without the need for external synchronization. However, this comes at the cost of reduced performance, since synchronization involves additional overhead.

In general, it is recommended to use an ArrayList or a LinkedList in most cases, since they are more efficient and the additional synchronization provided by Vector is not usually needed. However, if you need to use a thread-safe list in a multithreaded environment, a Vector may be a good choice.

Like ArrayList and LinkedList, Vector is a generic class, which means that you can specify the type of elements that it stores. In the example above, we create a Vector of String objects, so we use the syntax Vector<String> names = new Vector<>();. This helps to ensure type safety and prevent runtime errors.

Stack:

In Java, a stack is a Last In First Out (LIFO) data structure that is implemented using a class. Here's an example of a stack class in Java:

```
import java.util.ArrayList;
class Stack {
ArrayList<Object> stack = new ArrayList<Object>();
// Push an element onto the stack
void push(Object element) {
stack.add(element);
}
// Pop an element off the stack
Object pop() {
if (stack.isEmpty()) {
return null;
}
return stack.remove(stack.size() - 1);
}
```

```
// Return the top element of the stack

Object peek() {

if (stack.isEmpty()) {

return null;

}

return stack.get(stack.size() - 1);

}

// Return the size of the stack

int size() {

return stack.size();

}

// Check if the stack is empty

boolean isEmpty() {

return stack.isEmpty();

}

}
```

To use this stack class, you can create a stack object and call the various methods to add elements to the stack, remove elements from the stack, and check the size and status of the stack. Here's an example of how you might use the stack class:

```
Stack stack = new Stack();

// Push some elements onto the stack

stack.push("Hello");

stack.push("World");

stack.push(123);

// Print the size of the stack

System.out.println("Stack size: " + stack.size()); // Output: "Stack size: 3"

// Peek at the top element of the stack
```

```java
System.out.println("Top element: " + stack.peek()); // Output: "Top element: 123"

// Pop an element off the stack

Object element = stack.pop();

System.out.println("Popped element: " + element); // Output: "Popped element: 123"

// Check if the stack is empty

if (stack.isEmpty()) {

System.out.println("Stack is empty");

} else {

System.out.println("Stack is not empty");

} // Output: "Stack is not empty"
```

A stack is a linear data structure that stores items in a Last-In/First-Out (LIFO) manner. In other words, the last element added to the stack will be the first one to be removed.

Here is an example of a stack implementation in Java:

```java
import java.util.ArrayList;

public class Stack {

private ArrayList<Object> elements;

public Stack() {

this.elements = new ArrayList<Object>();

}

public void push(Object item) {

elements.add(item);

}

public Object pop() {

if (elements.isEmpty()) {

throw new EmptyStackException();

}
```

```
return elements.remove(elements.size() - 1);
}
public Object peek() {
if (elements.isEmpty()) {
throw new EmptyStackException();
}
return elements.get(elements.size() - 1);
}
public boolean isEmpty() {
return elements.isEmpty();
}
public int size() {
return elements.size();
}
}
```

To use this stack, you can do the following:

```
Stack stack = new Stack();
stack.push("apple");
stack.push("banana");
stack.push("orange");
System.out.println(stack.pop()); // orange
System.out.println(stack.pop()); // banana
System.out.println(stack.pop()); // apple
```

This stack implementation uses an ArrayList to store the elements, but you could also use a linked list or an array to implement a stack.

Set:

A set is a collection of unique elements. In Java, the Set interface is a member of the java.util package and extends the Collection interface. It is an unordered collection, meaning that the elements are not stored in a specific order, and it does not allow duplicate elements.

Here is an example of a set implementation in Java using the HashSet class, which is a common implementation of the Set interface that uses a hash table for storage:

```
import java.util.HashSet;

import java.util.Set;

public class Example {

public static void main(String[] args) {

Set<String> set = new HashSet<>();

set.add("apple");

set.add("banana");

set.add("orange");

set.add("apple"); // this element will not be added to the set because sets do not allow duplicates

System.out.println(set); // [orange, banana, apple] (the order may vary)

}

}
```

To use this set, you can add elements to it using the add() method and check if it contains an element using the contains() method:

```
Set<String> set = new HashSet<>();

set.add("apple");

set.add("banana");

if (set.contains("apple")) {

System.out.println("The set contains the element 'apple'.");

}
```

You can also remove elements from the set using the remove() method and iterate over the elements using an iterator obtained from the iterator() method.

There are several other implementation classes of the Set interface in Java, such as LinkedHashSet and TreeSet. These classes offer different performance characteristics and additional features. For example, a

TreeSet stores the elements in a sorted order, while a LinkedHashSet maintains the order in which the elements were added to the set.

HashSet:

A HashSet is a implementation of the Set interface in Java that uses a hash table for storage. It offers constant time performance for the basic operations (add, remove, contains and size), assuming the hash function disperses the elements properly among the buckets.

Here is an example of how to use a HashSet in Java:

```
import java.util.HashSet;

import java.util.Set;

public class Example {

public static void main(String[] args) {

Set<String> set = new HashSet<>();

set.add("apple");

set.add("banana");

set.add("orange");

set.add("apple"); // this element will not be added to the set because sets do not allow duplicates

System.out.println(set.size()); // 3

System.out.println(set.contains("apple")); // true

System.out.println(set.contains("mango")); // false

set.remove("banana");

System.out.println(set.size()); // 2

System.out.println(set.contains("banana")); // false

}

}
```

In this example, we create a HashSet of strings and add some elements to it. Then we use the size() method to get the number of elements in the set, the contains() method to check if the set contains a specific element, and the remove() method to remove an element from the set.

Note that the HashSet does not guarantee the order of the elements, so the output of the toString() method, which is used by println() to print the set, may not be the same as the order in which the elements were added.

LinkedHashSet:

A LinkedHashSet is a implementation of the Set interface in Java that extends HashSet and maintains a doubly-linked list running through all of its entries. This linked list defines the iteration ordering, which is the order in which elements were inserted into the set (insertion-order).

Here is an example of how to use a LinkedHashSet in Java:

```
import java.util.LinkedHashSet;

import java.util.Set;

public class Example {

public static void main(String[] args) {

Set<String> set = new LinkedHashSet<>();

set.add("apple");

set.add("banana");

set.add("orange");

set.add("apple"); // this element will not be added to the set because sets do not allow duplicates

System.out.println(set); // [apple, banana, orange] (the order is preserved)

}

}
```

In this example, we create a LinkedHashSet of strings and add some elements to it. Then we use the toString() method to print the set, which prints the elements in the order in which they were added.

Note that, like HashSet, LinkedHashSet offers constant time performance for the basic operations (add, remove, contains and size), assuming the hash function disperses the elements properly among the buckets. However, LinkedHashSet provides iteration performance that is likely to be faster than that of HashSet, because the iteration order is guaranteed to be the insertion order.

You can also create a LinkedHashSet that orders its elements according to their natural ordering or according to a Comparator provided at set creation time. To do this, you can use the appropriate constructor:

```
// natural ordering

Set<Integer> set = new LinkedHashSet<>(16, 0.75f, true);

// custom comparator
```

```
Set<String> set = new LinkedHashSet<>(16, 0.75f, true, new MyStringComparator());
```

TreeSet:

A TreeSet is a collection in Java that stores elements in a sorted and ascending order. It is implemented using a tree data structure, and it extends the AbstractSet class and implements the NavigableSet interface.

Here is an example of how to use a TreeSet in Java:

```
import java.util.TreeSet;

public class Main {

public static void main(String[] args) {

// Create a TreeSet

TreeSet<Integer> numbers = new TreeSet<>();

// Add elements to the TreeSet

numbers.add(5);

numbers.add(2);

numbers.add(8);

numbers.add(1);

numbers.add(7);

// Print the TreeSet

System.out.println(numbers); // Output: [1, 2, 5, 7, 8]

}

}
```

In this example, we create a TreeSet called numbers and add five elements to it. When we print the TreeSet, it prints the elements in a sorted and ascending order.

Map:

A Map is an interface in Java that stores key-value pairs and maps keys to values. It is part of the java.util package and is implemented by various classes, such as HashMap, TreeMap, and LinkedHashMap.

Here is an example of how to use a Map in Java:

```
import java.util.HashMap;
```

```java
import java.util.Map;

public class Main {

public static void main(String[] args) {

// Create a Map

Map<String, String> map = new HashMap<>();

// Add key-value pairs to the Map

map.put("key1", "value1");

map.put("key2", "value2");

map.put("key3", "value3");

// Print the Map

System.out.println(map); // Output: {key1=value1, key2=value2, key3=value3}

// Get the value for a specific key

String value = map.get("key2");

System.out.println(value); // Output: value2

// Check if the Map contains a specific key

boolean containsKey = map.containsKey("key3");

System.out.println(containsKey); // Output: true

// Check if the Map contains a specific value

boolean containsValue = map.containsValue("value1");

System.out.println(containsValue); // Output: true

// Remove a key-value pair from the Map

map.remove("key1");

}

}
```

In this example, we create a Map called map and add three key-value pairs to it. We then print the Map, get the value for a specific key, check if the Map contains a specific key or value, and remove a key-value pair from the Map.

HashMap:

HashMap is a class in Java that implements the Map interface and stores key-value pairs. It is part of the java.util package and uses a hash table to store the elements.

Here is an example of how to use a HashMap in Java:

```
import java.util.HashMap;

import java.util.Map;

public class Main {

public static void main(String[] args) {

// Create a HashMap

Map<String, String> map = new HashMap<>();

// Add key-value pairs to the HashMap

map.put("key1", "value1");

map.put("key2", "value2");

map.put("key3", "value3");

// Print the HashMap

System.out.println(map); // Output: {key1=value1, key2=value2, key3=value3}

// Get the value for a specific key

String value = map.get("key2");

System.out.println(value); // Output: value2

// Check if the HashMap contains a specific key

boolean containsKey = map.containsKey("key3");

System.out.println(containsKey); // Output: true

// Check if the HashMap contains a specific value

boolean containsValue = map.containsValue("value1");

System.out.println(containsValue); // Output: true

// Remove a key-value pair from the HashMap
```

```
map.remove("key1");
}
}
```

In this example, we create a HashMap called map and add three key-value pairs to it. We then print the HashMap, get the value for a specific key, check if the HashMap contains a specific key or value, and remove a key-value pair from the HashMap.

LinkedHashMap:

LinkedHashMap is a class in Java that extends the HashMap class and maintains a linked list of the entries in the map, in the order in which they were inserted. It is part of the java.util package and implements the Map interface.

Here is an example of how to use a LinkedHashMap in Java:

```
import java.util.LinkedHashMap;
import java.util.Map;
public class Main {
public static void main(String[] args) {
// Create a LinkedHashMap
Map<String, String> map = new LinkedHashMap<>();
// Add key-value pairs to the LinkedHashMap
map.put("key1", "value1");
map.put("key2", "value2");
map.put("key3", "value3");
// Print the LinkedHashMap
System.out.println(map); // Output: {key1=value1, key2=value2, key3=value3}
// Get the value for a specific key
String value = map.get("key2");
System.out.println(value); // Output: value2
// Check if the LinkedHashMap contains a specific key
boolean containsKey = map.containsKey("key3")
```

```
System.out.println(containsKey); // Output: true
// Check if the LinkedHashMap contains a specific value
boolean containsValue = map.containsValue("value1");
System.out.println(containsValue); // Output: true
// Remove a key-value pair from the LinkedHashMap
map.remove("key1");
}
}
```

In this example, we create a LinkedHashMap called map and add three key-value pairs to it. We then print the LinkedHashMap, get the value for a specific key, check if the LinkedHashMap contains a specific key or value, and remove a key-value pair from the LinkedHashMap.

One of the main differences between a LinkedHashMap and a HashMap is that the LinkedHashMap maintains the insertion order of the elements, while the HashMap does not. This means that when you iterate over the keys or values of a LinkedHashMap, they will be in the same order in which they were inserted.

TreeMap:

TreeMap implements the Map interface and stores key-value pairs in a sorted, ascending order. It is part of the java.util package and is implemented using a tree data structure.

Here is an example of how to use a TreeMap in Java:

```
import java.util.TreeMap;
import java.util.Map;
public class Main {
public static void main(String[] args) {
// Create a TreeMap
Map<String, String> map = new TreeMap<>();
// Add key-value pairs to the TreeMap
map.put("key1", "value1");
map.put("key2", "value2");
map.put("key3", "value3");
```

```
// Print the TreeMap
System.out.println(map); // Output: {key1=value1, key2=value2, key3=value3}
// Get the value for a specific key
String value = map.get("key2");
System.out.println(value); // Output: value2
// Check if the TreeMap contains a specific key
boolean containsKey = map.containsKey("key3");
System.out.println(containsKey); // Output: true
// Check if the TreeMap contains a specific value
boolean containsValue = map.containsValue("value1");
System.out.println(containsValue); // Output: true
// Remove a key-value pair from the TreeMap
map.remove("key1");
}
}
```

In this example, we create a TreeMap called map and add three key-value pairs to it. We then print the TreeMap, get the value for a specific key, check if the TreeMap contains a specific key or value, and remove a key-value pair from the TreeMap.

One of the main differences between a TreeMap and a HashMap is that the TreeMap stores the elements in a sorted, ascending order, while the HashMap does not. This means that when you iterate over the keys or values of a TreeMap, they will be in a sorted order.

HashMap internal working:

A HashMap in Java is a hash table-based implementation of the Map interface. It stores key-value pairs and uses a hash function to map the keys to their corresponding values in the hash table.

The HashMap class uses an array as the underlying data structure, and each element in the array is a LinkedList or a TreeMap. When you add a key-value pair to a HashMap, the hash function is used to calculate the hash code of the key, and the hash code is used to determine the index at which the key-value pair should be stored in the array.

If two keys have the same hash code, they are said to have collided, and the HashMap handles the collision by storing both key-value pairs in the same index in the array, using a LinkedList or a TreeMap depending on the number of collisions.

When you try to retrieve a value for a specific key from a HashMap, the hash function is used again to calculate the hash code of the key, and the HashMap uses the hash code to determine the index in the array where the key-value pair is stored. It then searches the LinkedList or TreeMap at that index for the key-value pair and returns the value if it is found.

The HashMap class provides constant-time performance for the basic operations (get and put), assuming the hash function distributes the keys uniformly in the array. However, the performance can degrade if there are a large number of collisions, as the HashMap may have to search through a long LinkedList or TreeMap to find the key-value pair.

Hashtable:

Hashtable is a class in Java that implements the Map interface and stores key-value pairs. It is part of the java.util package and uses a hash table to store the elements.

Here is an example of how to use a Hashtable in Java:

```
import java.util.Hashtable;

import java.util.Map;

public class Main {

public static void main(String[] args) {

// Create a Hashtable

Map<String, String> map = new Hashtable<>();

// Add key-value pairs to the Hashtable

map.put("key1", "value1");

map.put("key2", "value2");

map.put("key3", "value3");

// Print the Hashtable

System.out.println(map); // Output: {key1=value1, key2=value2, key3=value3}

// Get the value for a specific key

String value = map.get("key2");

System.out.println(value); // Output: value2

// Check if the Hashtable contains a specific key
```

```
boolean containsKey = map.containsKey("key3");
System.out.println(containsKey); // Output: true
// Check if the Hashtable contains a specific value
boolean containsValue = map.containsValue("value1");
System.out.println(containsValue); // Output: true
// Remove a key-value pair from the Hashtable
map.remove("key1");
}
}
```

In this example, we create a Hashtable called map and add three key-value pairs to it. We then print the Hashtable, get the value for a specific key, check if the Hashtable contains a specific key or value, and remove a key-value pair from the Hashtable.

One of the main differences between a Hashtable and a HashMap is that the Hashtable is synchronized, while the HashMap is not. This means that the Hashtable is thread-safe, while the HashMap is not. However, the HashMap is generally faster than the Hashtable due to its lack of synchronization.

Iteration collection:

There are several ways to iterate over the elements in a collection in Java. One way is to use the for-each loop, which was introduced in Java 5.

Here is an example of how to use the for-each loop to iterate over the elements in a List in Java:

```
import java.util.ArrayList;
import java.util.List;
public class Main {
public static void main(String[] args) {
// Create a List
List<String> list = new ArrayList<>();
// Add elements to the List
list.add("apple");
list.add("banana");
```

```
list.add("cherry");
// Iterate over the elements in the List
for (String element : list) {
System.out.println(element); // Output: apple, banana, cherry
}
}
}
```

In this example, we create a List called list and add three elements to it. We then use the for-each loop to iterate over the elements in the List and print them.

Another way to iterate over the elements in a collection is to use an iterator. An iterator is an object that allows you to iterate over a collection and access its elements one by one.

Here is an example of how to use an iterator to iterate over the elements in a Set in Java:

```
import java.util.HashSet;
import java.util.Iterator;
import java.util.Set;
public class Main {
public static void main(String[] args) {
// Create a Set
Set<String> set = new HashSet<>();
// Add elements to the Set
set.add("apple");
set.add("banana");
set.add("cherry");
// Get an iterator for the Set
Iterator<String> iterator = set.iterator();
// Iterate over the elements in the Set
while (iterator.hasNext()) {
```

```
String element = iterator.next();
System.out.println(element); // Output: apple, banana, cherry
}
}
}
```

In this example, we create a Set called set and add three elements to it. We then use the iterator() method to get an iterator for the Set, and use the hasNext() and next() methods of the iterator to iterate over the elements in the Set and print them.

ListIterator is an interface in Java that extends the Iterator interface and allows you to iterate over the elements of a List in either direction (forward or backward). It is part of the java.util package and is implemented by various classes, such as ArrayList and LinkedList.

Here is an example of how to use a ListIterator in Java:

```
import java.util.ArrayList;
import java.util.List;
import java.util.ListIterator;
public class Main {
public static void main(String[] args) {
// Create a List
List<String> list = new ArrayList<>();
// Add elements to the List
list.add("apple");
list.add("banana");
list.add("cherry");
// Get a ListIterator for the List
ListIterator<String> iterator = list.listIterator();
// Iterate over the elements of the List in the forward direction
System.out.println("Forward iteration:");
while (iterator.hasNext()) {
```

```
String element = iterator.next();
System.out.println(element);
}
// Output: apple, banana, cherry
// Iterate over the elements of the List in the backward direction
System.out.println("\nBackward iteration:");
while (iterator.hasPrevious()) {
String element = iterator.previous();
System.out.println(element);
}
// Output: cherry, banana, apple
}
}
```

In this example, we create a List called list and add three elements to it. We then get a ListIterator for the List and use it to iterate over the elements of the List in the forward and backward directions.

One of the main advantages of using a ListIterator is that it allows you to iterate over the elements of a List in either direction, while a regular Iterator only allows you

Contents

Printed by Libri Plureos GmbH in Hamburg,
Germany